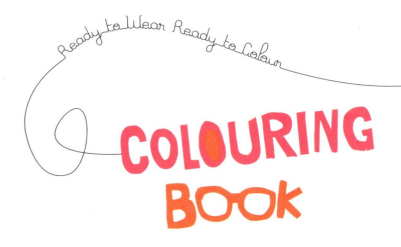

Ready to Wear Ready to Colour

COLOURING

BOOK

© 2011 Éditions Glénat and
Fondation Pierre Bergé -Yves Saint Laurent

First published in Great Britain 2011 by Walker Books Ltd
87 Vauxhall Walk, London SE11 5HJ

10 9 8 7 6 5 4 3 2 1

Published by arrangement with Éditions Glénat, Grenoble, France

This book has been typeset in Anke Sans

Printed in Italy

British Library Cataloguing in Publication Data:
a catalogue record for this book is available from the British Library

ISBN 978–1–4063–3883–6

www.walker.co.uk

WALKER BOOKS

AND SUBSIDIARIES

LONDON • BOSTON • SYDNEY • AUCKLAND

LONG LIVE THE MODERN WOMAN!

Yves Saint Laurent's first *Rive Gauche* boutique opened in 1966 at 21, rue de Tournon in Paris.

SAINT LAURENT
rive gauche

Modern colours forever!

Use the hues of Yves Saint Laurent's boutique as your inspiration to bring colour to these four sketches.

SAINT LAURENT
rive gauche

The *Rive Gauche* silhouette

Use the vibrant tones chosen by Yves Saint Laurent to bring warmth to these thoroughly modern dresses.

You can cinch the waist of this dress with a gold chain belt as shown on the model below.

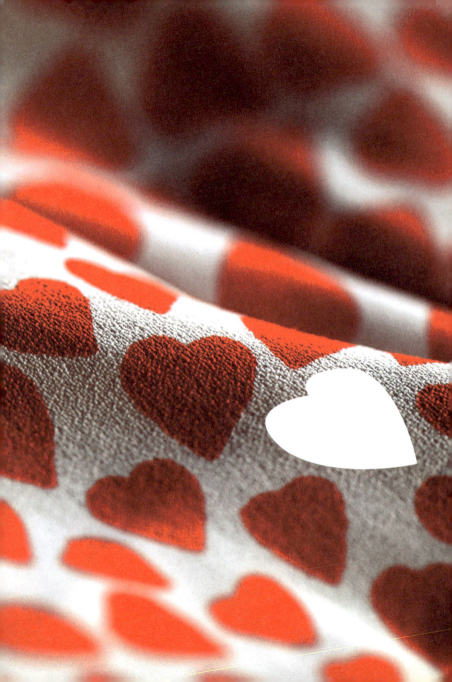

Love it!

Yves Saint Laurent celebrates life and love! Red hearts are at the core of this fabric design. Now it's up to you to create your own multicoloured heart print.

longueur Tot du *Blouse* 439 GABY

Jupe 275

de la

Jupe 80cm   3 cm Taffe

Robe   5 cm

rouge

                                      perse
                                      uni

                                          — T

5 cm

3 cm

                — Jupe 5
                avec 1/2
                carreau
                la Taill

Ceinture
de Taffetas

                                  24cm
                                  de vr

                              5cm d

Romantic ruffles and rich velvet —
dreamy dresses for young romantics.

After you've coloured in these designs,
put yourself in the designer's shoes
and add your own descriptions next
to the outfits.

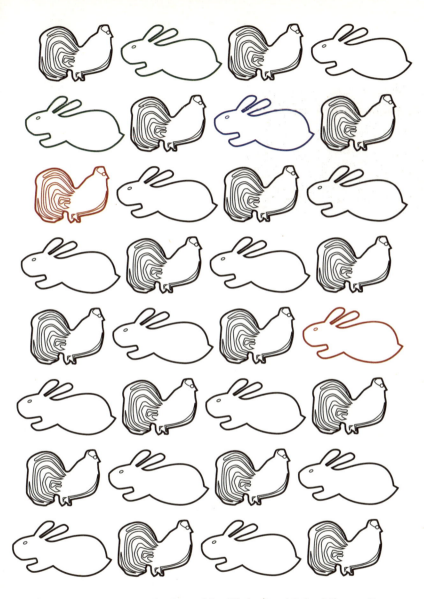

Welcome to a magical world with just a hint of the naïve.

Bring life to this joyful menagerie by using different colours and patterns
for each line.

SAINT LAURENT
rive gauche

Black and white

Yves Saint Laurent's tuxedo,
le smoking, created the first
link between the worlds of haute
couture and ready−to−wear.
Recreate its elegant spirit using
only black and white to colour
in this page.

The original design by
Yves Saint Laurent.

The confident
feminine woman

Join the dots to create
a silhouette for this
design and once you
have an outline, use
these swatches as
your colour guide.

Robe   col, poignets

Design a small hat for this model
to complete her outfit.

The summer of '67

There are two spaces in this collection. Create two new looks in summery colours so that the catwalk is complete.

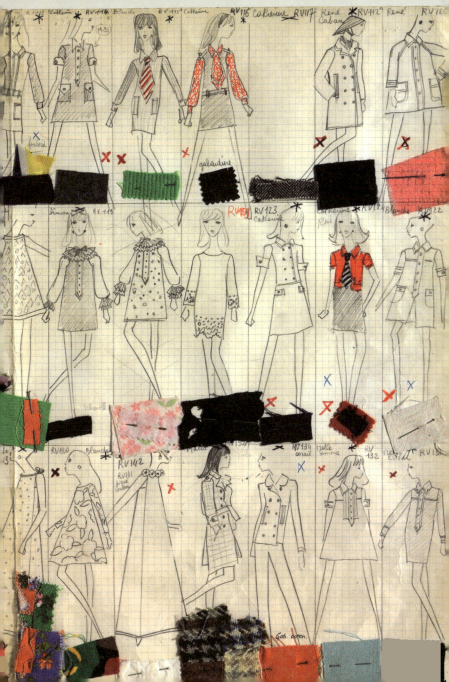

RV334 RV342 RV350 RV349 RV348 RV

RV159 RV336 RV357

RV300 RV333 RV347 RV358 RV

You, the designer!

Copy the patterns on the swatches under each design and have fun adding colour to this line—up of outfits.

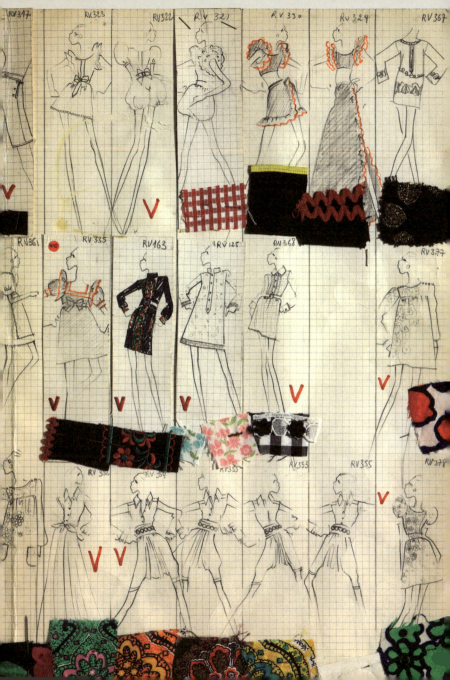

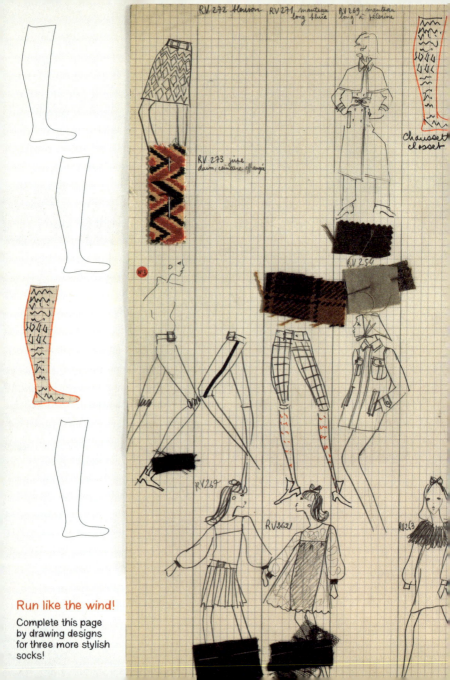

RV 272 blouson

RV 271 manteau long pluie

RV 269 manteau long à pélérine

Chausset closset

RV 273 jupe daim, ceinture effangé

RV 254

RV 267

RV 262?

RV 263

Run like the wind!

Complete this page by drawing designs for three more stylish socks!

268 robe feutre

RV255

Pantalons

M. Fen

Robe Rayée
Closset

loden
brodé

RV381   RV382   RV384   RV3

RV383

Dotty about polka dots!

Add polka dots in every kind of
colour combination and have
some fun with these outfits.

© Sophie Carre

Forever rose

Trace over the lines of these flowers with a fine black felt tip,
then fill in the designs, swapping the colours: blue for the
flowers, pink for the leaves and green for the backgrounds.

© Sophie Cars

Draw a model for
this dress and
colour it in.

Bring back the colour to these
stripy dresses.

RV 342   RV 350   RV 349   RV 348

SAINT LAURENT
rive gauche

Kiss kiss!

Borrow your mum's
lipstick and add a
great big smack of
colour to these
pretty little mouths!
(Just don't forget to
ask first!)

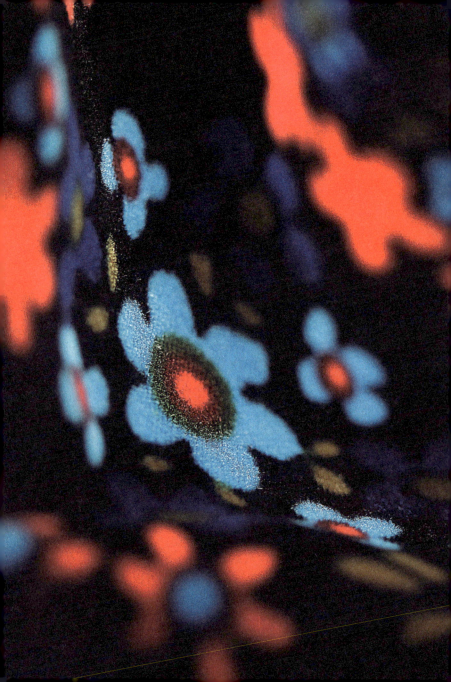

Carte blanche for the budding artist!
Let your creativity run wild and completely cover this page with flowers.

SAINT LAURENT
rive gauche

Long live stylish comfort!

The Saint Laurent *Rive Gauche* label offers women elegant, accessible clothing. Choose three seasonal shades to enrich these designs.

THE NIGHT IS FOR
PARTYING

PARTY ON! DRESSES AND DANCING FROM DUSK TILL DAWN!

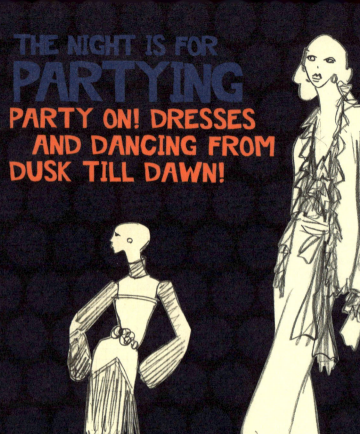

Princesses and dreamers, beautiful by night and day...

Bring back the smiles to the faces of these models. Bring back the colour so that the party can get started!

Flowers forever

It's up to you to fill the spaces
– use any colours you like!